THE BOONDOCKS

Because I Know You Don't Read the Newspaper

by Aaron McGruder

**Andrews McMeel
Publishing, LLC**

Kansas City

The Boondocks may be viewed on the Internet at:

www.boondocks.net

─── **ATTENTION: SCHOOLS AND BUSINESSES** ───

Andrews McMeel books are available at quantity discounts with bulk purchase for educational, business, or sales promotional use. For information, please write to: Special Sales Department, Andrews McMeel Publishing, LLC, 1130 Walnut Street, Kansas City, Missouri 64106

This book is dedicated to my parents, Elaine and Bill McGruder,
the first and still the best people in my life.

To my beautiful grandparents, Robert and Thelma Carrier.

To Robert Hord, Rhome Anderson, and Reginald Hudlin . . . my friends.

To the life and memory of Charles Schulz (I'll never get to call you "Sparky"), and to
Garry Trudeau, Berke Breathed, and Bill Watterson, for obvious reasons.

To Jeanne McCarty, Dr. Melinda Chateauvert, Dr. Ollie Johnson, and the
Afro-American Studies program at the University of Maryland for actually
teaching me something in school and then helping me get the hell out.

To the NABJ, Lonnae O'Neal Parker, Joann Lyons Wooten, Garry Howard, Chrisette Suter,
Johnnie Cochran, Tavis Smiley, and the Black media who helped spread the word.

To W. E. B. DuBois, Malcolm X, Bob Marley, Dr. Mary Frances Berry, Lawrence Guyot,
and all freedom fighters of yesterday, today, and especially tomorrow.

To Bob Johnson and Ward Connerly—great villains make great heroes.

To Stephen Barnes, "every Black person's lawyer."

To John McMeel, Kathy Andrews, Lee Salem, Bob Duffy, John Vivona, and all
those other folks at the syndicate for their hard work and faith . . . and
especially to Greg Melvin, Robert Hightower, and Pam Carr.

To Basheera James, Sharifa Foum, and Tony Miller—just for being wonderful people.

To the World-Famous Soul Controller Massive (DJ Book, DJ Stylus, Bushhead Ed, and DJ Mr. Elite).

To the hip-hop artists who used to teach Black people to love themselves . . . and the
few who still do.

To the fans at Boondocks.net and okayplayer.com.

To 'Stress, for helping me get my life back.

To my adopted godmother and the reason you're reading this book, Harriet Choice.

And to the person I love most in the whole world . . . my brother, Dedric.

Foreword

Race is the most fertile yet untapped realm for the creation of powerful storytelling.

Put another way, conflict is drama. Race is where the conflict that is drama's bubblin' crude can be found in widest abundance, and down to almost limitless depths.

But instead of mining the racial strata for the new, vital stories that racism presently withholds, or even digging for old, untold ones, today's popular storytellers are often more likely to feed their audiences gentle fictions of interracial collegiality; Black people and white people collaborating indifferently across racial lines, as though under the terms of an unearned truce.

Watch any number of TV shows or movies to view this trend in action: See the white girl with the mothering, Black roommate, or the Black guy whose best friend is the hip, smart-ass white guy. Hip-hop, certainly, seems to be in the throes of this tendency, given the increased number and prominence of both white rappers and fans, but, perhaps even more, given the current and increasing number of white, so-called rap-rockers.

Many, considering the tragedies from which Black people have risen—but perhaps, even more, the barbarism from which white people have come—see this lack of racial differentiation as progress. "Why do we have to keep bringing up the past?" they ask.

Because "those who cannot remember the past are condemned to repeat it," answers philosopher George Santayana. The truth of race's fundamental divisiveness and apparent permanence, no matter how harsh or unexpected, always makes better retelling than a jaw full of fantasy or wishful thinking about it.

Aaron McGruder, meanwhile, also thinks frankness in racial matters makes better punch lines. Of course, he's right. His commitment to candor in comedy is what makes *The Boondocks* the most potent new entry in the comic strip medium since the early 1970s, when Garry Trudeau first started smacking sacred cows in *Doonesbury*. It's what makes *The Boondocks* the most successful debut strip in the history of Universal Press Syndicate, which launched it in 160 newspapers on April 19, 1999, then grew that list to over 200 dailies by that year's end. (The syndicate had expected it to debut in, perhaps, 30 to 50 papers.)

It's also why, once having read *The Boondocks*, few are indifferent about it—if the small, but noteworthy number of newspapers that have canceled the strip is any indication. While the comic's premise is deftly straightforward, it is certainly not innocuous. As social construct, the tale of Huey and Riley Freeman—two prepubescent African-American males who leave Chicago's South side to live with their grandfather in the blindingly white suburb of Woodcrest—takes place right at the nexus of white American racial anxiety; that moment where their neighborhoods start *changing*: "changing" being code for "Black people are moving in."

What marks McGruder's sensibility as wonderfully perverse, though, is the way he, having set up that initial set of conditions, begins to drop in the details that will make it weirdly unravel, like a cartoon strip version of *The Sims*. In *The Boondocks*, the Freemans are just under twelve parsecs away from those cuddly, wide-eyed, Negro comic strip innocents we've grown to know and hate. Huey Freeman is a pint-sized, foot-high-Afro-wearing, razor-tongued Black revolutionary, and Riley is a half-pint-sized, platinum-coveting, foul-mouthed roughneck. Like Cain and Abel, they signify two long-standing, mutually opposed, vigorous traditions in the so-called Black community, clasped in uneasy, brotherly embrace.

Their foils? Their Southern, traditionalist grandfather, completing the symbolic triad of Black American modalities represented in the Freeman home: radical, integrationist, thug; a "biracial" girl, Jazmine DuBois; her Black father, Tom, and his white wife, Sarah, both lawyers; and Cindy, a white girl so clueless she has no idea why her request to touch Huey's "different . . . cool" hair (p. 73) returns the promise of a pummeling.

With the addition of a few more minor characters, McGruder then rudely impales everything from Jar-Jar Binks, *Star Wars* fandom, telemarketers, and the NAACP to Puff Daddy, Black Entertainment Television, and Santa Claus. Certainly the only comic strip in history to have a character deem the U.S. was built on "stolen land," advocate the formation of a local Klanwatch, and brutally dis Ward Connerly, *The Boondocks* avoids the boorishness to which others might sink by virtue of McGruder's light saber-sharp intelligence, the drollness of his drawing style, and the consistency of his characters and their universe.

And, oh yeah: It's mad funny. My conversion came early in the strip's history, the moment Huey, meeting Jazmine for the first time, offhandedly called her "Mariah," as in "Carey." I think I screamed till my sides ached.

Hey: Truth hurts.

Free Jolly Jenkins!

Harry Allen,
Hip-Hop Activist and Media Assassin,
Harlem, New York
May 2000

8

11

13

14

"STAR WARS" FANATICS REJOICE!

The day we've waited countless years for has finally arrived. Today, in what many believe to be the most important day in cinema history, "STAR WARS: EPISODE 1" opens in theaters across the country. I think Huey and Riley speak for "Star Wars" aficionados all over when they say...

WELL, RILEY, YOU'VE JUST SEEN THE MOST ANTICIPATED MOVIE OF ALL TIME. WHAT DID YOU THINK?

JACKSON WAS TASIC! AN OSCAR-NING PERFORMANCE!

THIS WHOLE PLACE IS MINE FOR THE TAKING! **ALL MINE!!** THE CRIMINAL MASTERMIND "**RILEY ESCOBAR**" IS HERE TO RUN THINGS!!!

CHIEF MAFIOSO THUG KINGPIN "**RILEY ESCO**" IS NOW IN CHARGE! I'M PACKIN' HEAT, I HATE COPS, I DON'T FEAR JAIL! **WHAT**!!! HOLD ON TO YOUR JEWELS 'CAUSE RILEY IS TAKIN' YOUR LOOT - **BELIEVE DAT**!!

"PLAYA HATAS **GET AWAY** OR MY LEAD WILL SPRAY..."

YOU KNOW, IT MIGHT HELP IF YOU **DIDN'T** SHOUT YOUR NEFARIOUS PLANS FROM A HILLTOP.

YOU AND I ARE **OBVIOUSLY** NOT LISTENING TO THE SAME RAP MUSIC.

TRUE. I'M ALLERGIC TO STUDIO GANGSTERS.

YES?

HI!! I'M CINDY FROM DOWN THE STREET! WELCOME TO WOODCREST!!!

WOW, CAN I GET YOUR AUTOGRAPH? I BET YOU'RE FAMOUS. YOU LOOK LIKE SOMEONE FAMOUS.

WHO?

YOU KNOW... THOSE RAPPER GUYS... **HEY**, DO YOU KNOW **PUFFY**?

GOODBYE, CINDY.

23

24

26

28

32

40

OK, PSYCHO "STAR WARS" GUY, I HOLD IN MY HAND A COPY OF EPISODE ONE'S FINAL SCRIPT DRAFT. SNAP OUT OF THIS DENIAL OR I WILL READ IT ALOUD FROM BEGINNING TO END. PREPARE TO BE SUBJECTED TO TWO HOURS OF DEPLORABLE SCREENWRITING!!

I LOVED THE THICK ASIAN ACCENTS...

Two hours of deplorable screen-writing later…

UHHHGH. JAR JAR REALLY DOES SOUND LIKE MUSHMOUTH FROM "FAT ALBERT."

I THINK HE'S BACK TO NORMAL.

I DON'T THINK HE EVER WAS NORMAL.

I CAN'T BELIEVE I WAITED IN LINE FOR OVER A YEAR FOR "STAR WARS" AND IT STUNK.

I KNOW IT'S TOUGH.

IT'S NOT FAIR. A **YEAR** OF MY LIFE. **I DEMAND RESTITUTION**!!

PERHAPS YOU SHOULD CONSIDER LEGAL ACTION.

HEY... THAT'S NOT A BAD IDEA — LOST WAGES, MENTAL DISTRESS — I COULD SELL SOME OF MY "STAR WARS" TOYS AND HIRE A LAWYER!

HOW MUCH IS YOUR COLLECTION WORTH?

WHO KNOWS? THREE OR FOUR HUNDRED THOUSAND...

WHY NOT SELL IT ALL AND HIRE JOHNNIE COCHRAN FOR A WEEK?

DO YOU THINK HE WOULD TAKE THE CASE?

SO YOU'RE SAYING I SHOULD SELL OFF MY WHOLE "STAR WARS" COLLECTION, HIRE JOHNNIE COCHRAN, AND SUE GEORGE LUCAS FOR A DISAPPOINTING MOVIE.

IF YOU'RE LUCKY, HE'LL DO ONE OF THOSE CLEVER "IF IT DOESN'T FIT..." RHYMES IN HIS CLOSING ARGUMENT.

LIKE, "THE MOVIE STINKS CAUSE OF JAR JAR BINKS."

"THE MOVIE'S WACK, NEEDS MORE SAM JACK."

"THIS MOVIE'S LIKE VALIUM, BLAME GEORGE AND MCCALLUM."

"THE MOVIE'S TRASH, GEORGE OWES US CASH."

WOW, SO YOU REALLY THINK THIS WILL WORK, HUH?

NOT A CHANCE. YOU NEED TO GET A LIFE AND LET IT GO, CHIEF. SORRY.

41

44

47

49

51

55

Panel 1: WELL, SCHOOL STARTS IN A FEW DAYS.

YEP.

Panel 2: YOU'RE HANDLING THIS RATHER WELL.

SHOOT, WHY SHOULD I CARE?

Panel 3: WELL, I JUST THOUGHT THAT YOU HATED SCHOOL ...

WHAT? YOU THOUGHT I WAS **GOING**?!

Panel 4: YOU WON'T BELIEVE THIS. GUESS WHAT THE NAME OF OUR NEW SCHOOL IS.

WHAT?

Panel 5: **J. EDGAR HOOVER** ELEMENTARY!! MADNESS, RIGHT?

WHAT'S THE BIG DEAL?

Panel 6: I MEAN, WHAT KIND OF SICK JOKE IS FATE TRYING TO PLAY HERE? I CAN'T GO TO A SCHOOL NAMED AFTER HOOVER!

WHATEVER, MAN.

Panel 7: NEVER MIND, YOU WOULDN'T KNOW J. EDGAR HOOVER FROM J.J. EVANS.

THAT AIN'T TRUE. I LIKE "GOOD TIMES."

Panel 8:  I'VE DECIDED SCHOOL IS FOR SUCKAS. I'M NOT GOING.

SCHOOL IS NOT FOR SUCKAS, RILEY.

Panel 9:  BUT YOU DON'T WANT TO GO EITHER ...

BUT I HAVE A CAUSE. THAT'S DIFFERENT. I BREAK RULES FOR THE GREATER GOOD.

Panel 10:  WELL THEN, **I** GOT A CAUSE, TOO.

REALLY? WHAT?

Panel 11:  I DON'T KNOW — SAVE THE WHALES, FREE MANDELA, WHATEVER — LET ME BREAK SOME RULES, TOO ...

68

Here we find the radical scholar and future voice of Black America HUEY FREEMAN diligently working on his first book. An expansive and thorough text, it will offer a critical analysis of the black neoconservative movement and its most famous champion.

Ward Connerly Should Be Beaten by Raekwon the Chef With a Spiked Bat
A Critical Look at Black Conservatives by Huey Freeman

As the brilliant young author reconsiders his title, he confronts the same dilemma as so many Black writers before him — choosing his audience. Raekwon, a name easily recognized by anyone affiliated with the hip-hop culture, will undoubtedly be lost on the society at large, including influential academic and political circles ...

Will Huey alienate the masses with obscure references? Can he broaden the scope of his work without corrupting its cultural integrity and unyielding radical tone? Can he discover the elusive middle ground between Frances Cress Welsing and Henry Louis Gates Jr.? Oh, we do not envy the difficult task facing poor Huey ...

Ward Connerly Is a Boot-Licking Uncle Tom
A Critical Look at Black Conservatives by Huey Freeman

Way to go, Huey! Everyone knows what a boot-licking Uncle Tom is! The ability to transcend cultural barriers is the mark of a great communicator. Keep this up and you'll be on "Charlie Rose" in no time!

JAZMINE IS AT HER GRAND-MOTHER'S, HUEY. WE'RE OFF TO LOS ANGELES FOR SOME GOOD OLD-FASHIONED NAACP NONVIOLENT SOCIAL PROTEST!

IS THAT RIGHT?

SEE, I'M PART OF THE TEAM THAT IS PROTESTING THE UNDER-REPRESENTATION OF BLACKS IN TELEVISION AND FILM THIS YEAR. WE'RE FIGHTING THE HOLLYWOOD WHITE-OUT!!

AND **I'M** PART OF THE TEAM THAT IS CALLING FOR THE CANCELLATION OF THE CURRENT BLACK SHOWS WE FIND OFFENSIVE — WHICH IS JUST ABOUT ALL OF THEM!

INTERESTING. SO WHO'S PART OF THE TEAM THAT WORKS PROACTIVELY TO INCREASE OPPORTUNITIES FOR BLACK WRITERS, HELP IN THE DEVELOPMENT OF BLACK PRO-JECTS, AND WORK OUTSIDE OF OUTDATED REACTIONARY PROTEST STRATEGIES?

HONEY, WILL THAT FIT ON A PICKET SIGN?

IT'S DOUBTFUL ...

WELL, NEVER MIND THEN ...

74

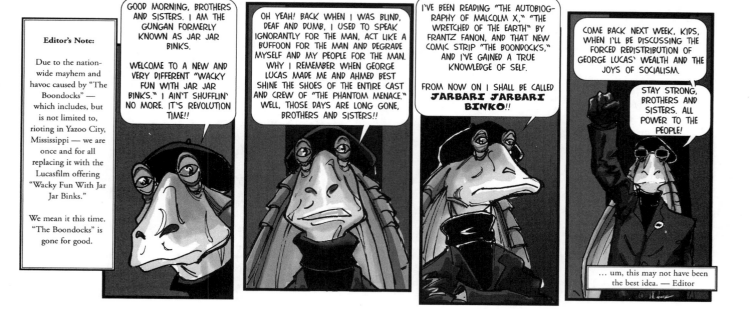

79

83

85

Woodcrest Tim...
streetsign Van...
Strikes Aga...

Dozens wonder...
will I get ma...

were all quite vocal in ...
...pposition to the renam...
...eir streets. "What the h...
...t anyway?" "I don't want ...
...growing up on Xzibit...
...es include Rza Blvd, H...
...ardcore Street.

No Suspec...
...say Police...
...mmissioner Gorda...

however, Detect...
...uick to point out t...
...re are no suspects ...
...hysical evidence,...
...e "actively pursui...
...y strong leads."

OK, IT LOOKS LIKE THE COPS ARE LEAVING.

I KNEW I SHOULDN'T HAVE NAMED THAT LAST STREET AFTER ME.

HAVE YOU PICKED A HALLOWEEN COSTUME?

I DON'T CELEBRATE EVIL.

HALLOWEEN ISN'T EVIL, IT'S FUN. DON'T YOU LIKE CANDY?

I CAN BUY CANDY AT THE STORE.

WELL, WHILE YOU'RE THERE, SEE IF YOU CAN BUY A CHILDHOOD. BYE.

YEAH? WELL, UH ...

OUCH.

HEY HUEY? DO YOU LIKE MY HALLOWEEN COSTUME? GUESS WHO I AM?

GOODNESS, CINDY, IS THAT YOU?

CALL ME SNOOP DOGG — WASSAP WIT` YOU, HOMEY?

YOUR PARENTS MUST BE SO PROUD ...

CHECK THIS OUT, "I DON'T **LUV** THAT TRICK, I DON'T **LUV** THAT TREAT ..."

EPILOGUE ...

Riley "Escobar" Freeman, though never actually charged with any criminal act, was nonetheless vilified in Woodcrest for years to come, much to his delight.

Cindy McPhearson was sentenced to one evening without supper, three hours with a therapist, and two weeks of private art classes in the hopes that she would learn to express herself in a more appropriate manner. She remains unrepentant.

The Black Entertainment Network was sued by the McPhearson family for "contributing to the delinquency of Cindy McPhearson." Attempts to settle out of court in exchange for free minutes on the Psychic Friends Hotline were declined by the plaintiff. The case is still pending.

95

97

98

99

100

103

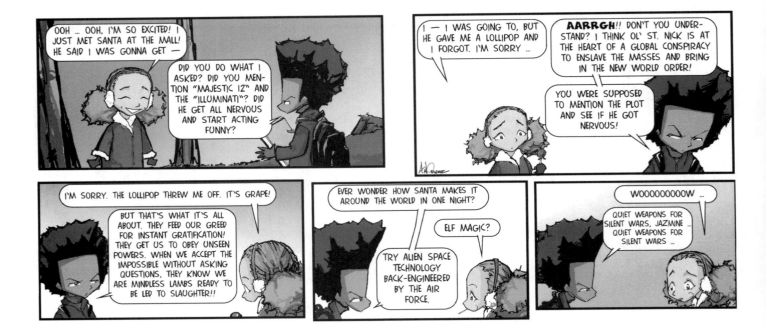

108

110

THE DAY AFTER CHRISTMAS ...

... A HAPPY JAZMINE ...

... A VERY HAPPY JAZMINE ...

HEY JAZMINE!!

HERE. I GOT THIS FOR YOU. HOLD ONTO IT UNTIL AFTER THE NEW YEAR.

A GIFT FOR **ME**?! HUEY THAT'S SO **SWEET**!. WHAT IS IT?

IT'S NOT A GIFT. IT'S A WALKIE-TALKIE ...

LET'S SAY, FOR EXAMPLE, THAT ON NEW YEAR'S DAY, THE PANIC OF THE NEW MILLENNIUM COUPLED WITH MASSIVE ECONOMIC CRASHES CAUSE A TOTAL BREAKDOWN OF SOCIETAL ORDER, WHICH QUICKLY DEGRADES INTO RIOTING, LOOTING, GLOBAL CHAOS, AND ULTIMATELY THE DECLARATION OF A STATE OF EMERGENCY AND THE INDEFINITE SUSPENSION OF THE CONSTITUTION UNDER AN OPPRESSIVE MARTIAL LAW IMPOSED BY **FEMA**. **THEN** LET'S SAY THE WHOLE STATE OF CALIFORNIA IS LEVELED BY A MASSIVE EARTHQUAKE, WHILE THE REST OF THE PLANET IS COVERED IN RAIN, HAIL, SNOW, VOLCANIC ERUPTIONS, TSUNAMIS AND TYPHOONS, ALL WHILE MAN-EATING PREDATOR TRIBES OF EXTRATERRESTRIALS HAVE LANDED ON THE WHITE HOUSE LAWN AND LAID CLAIM TO THE PLANET EARTH ...

...PLUS, YOUR PHONE DOESN'T WORK 'CAUSE OF Y2K. YOU CAN USE THE WALKIE-TALKIE TO CONTACT ME FOR HELP. OK?

IS ALL THAT STUFF **REALLY** GOING TO HAPPEN?!

WHO KNOWS? BUT WITH ARMAGEDDON IT'S BETTER TO BE SAFE THAN SORRY.

OH. WELL, THANK YOU FOR THE THINGIE.

NO PROBLEM. HAVE A NICE DAY.

THE DAY AFTER CHRISTMAS ...

AN UNHAPPY JAZMINE ...

... A VERY, **VERY** UNHAPPY JAZMINE ...

(SIGH)

IT IS THE DAWN OF A NEW ERA ...

HUEY FREEMAN, RADICAL SCHOLAR OF THE NEW MILLENNIUM, TAKES IN THE VIEW OF THE NEXT CHAPTER IN HUMAN HISTORY AND PREPARES A STATEMENT ...

FULLY UNDERSTANDING THE WEIGHT OF THE MOMENT, HE SEEKS TO EXPRESS HIS FEELINGS OF EXCITEMENT, APPREHENSION AND AWE IN ONE SENTENCE OF PROFOUND MEANING THAT WILL RESONATE THROUGH THE YEARS AHEAD ...

SOMETHING WISE ... SOMETHING INSPIRING ...

SOMETHING **DEEP** ... GOTTA BE **DEEP** ...

ISN'T THIS **GREAT**, HUEY?! 2000 CAME AND THE WORLD DIDN'T GO **KABLOOOIE**!!!

I THOUGHT OF THAT ALREADY ... NOT **DEEP** ENOUGH ...

118

124

128